The 4 Cuties – Freundinnen

Oster Edition

Für meinen Ehemann

Alle in diesem Buch
enthaltenen Rechte sind der
Autorin vorbehalten.

Autorin/Cover/Bilder

Tanja M. Feiler

Die Cuties machen Urlaub

1. Vester SchöneCrlage –
Partner – Webseiten –
Bücher: Schon immer die
Kreise geschlossen; Ein
President.   Ein   erste
Ausgabe von Onkel Tom
´s Hütte – Ich habe dieses
nicht gelesen – Es ist
heute   dank
Geschichtsbuch, in dem
wir gerade lesen nicht die
jetzt LIVE … Der welcher
Gott   dazu   veranlasste
kommen zu müssen ist

der welcher das Wissen hat dass der Tag schon lange gekommen ist, der Tag als wir erkennen lernten das – sollte das noch nicht so sein – so wissen wir dennoch, wir sterben doch ni...cht, dennoch haben en viele erst erkannt – schlicht, warum bin ich stark und sage nein zum Tod. Durch WISSSSENSCHAFT, ist es Ihre Wissenschaft, ihr

Eigentum – nein wer
nicht diese nicht eigne
WISSENSCHAFT
wenigsten Respektiert, der
wird diese dann spätestens
auf einem Friedhof im
nicht eigene Sarg nutzen
wo DIESE/ER das tun wird
was er immer getan hat.
Seinen wertvollsten Besitz
wissenschaftlich korrekt
zu Grabe bringen und
dafür dem richtigen
Wissenden seinen Lohn
dafür geben wollen.

Den mächtigsten Mann austauschen muss nicht sein, kaum jemand weiß das es die vereinigten STAATEN wirklich gibt, es ist aber sehr logisch weil es nur einen – MÄCHTIGSTEN MANN GANZ OFFIZIELL TÄTSÄCHLICH GIBT. President Barack Hussein Obama

∞

Publishers - partners - Web pages - books: Always the circuits closed; A President. A first edition of Uncle Tom BB ´s hut - I have this not read - it is today thanks to history, in which we read not just now LIVE... What God do this caused is to come which has the knowledge that the day has long come, the day when we recognize learned that - should this not be - so we still know we don't die, yet have only detected many en - simple, why I am strong and say no to the death. By WISSSSENSCHAFT, it's your science, their property - who not this not good science is least respected, which is then at least in a cemetery in the not your own coffin use this where this\/ER will do what he has always done.

His most valuable possessions bring scientifically correct to the grave and for the right knowing his reward want to give.
Replace the most powerful man doesn't have to be, hardly anyone knows that the United States really is there, it is very logical because it's just a – most powerful man GANZ officially is in fact.

President Barack Hussein Obama

2.Post vom Presidenten

Hey, Tanja

Barack Obama   Apr 1 um 2:54 AM

An ich

Tanja --

In just the past few years, we've seen millions of previously uninsured people get the coverage they need. We've seen students graduate from high school at a higher rate than ever, and more Americans are finishing college than ever before. We've seen millions of people go back to work. We've got an agenda, and we know it works.

And that's what this party is all about, Tanja. Middle-class economics. Expanding opportunity.

We're facing our first big fundraising deadline of the year tonight at midnight, and we're going to need your help. We were told by our friends on the other side of the aisle that our actions would destroy the country -- and while it's clear that isn't happening, you can bet they aren't going to let up. I hope you'll pitch in $10 or whatever you can to keep moving this country forward.

Thanks for this, Tanja. More than anything, this is all about doing things that make people's lives better -- and we can do that together.

Barack Obama

3. Die Cuties fahren los

¡Felices Pascuas!

Besonders Danke ich meinem Mann